Original title:
Journey to Joyful Marriage

Copyright © 2024 Swan Charm
All rights reserved.

Author: Liina Liblikas
ISBN HARDBACK: 978-9916-89-205-3
ISBN PAPERBACK: 978-9916-89-206-0
ISBN EBOOK: 978-9916-89-207-7

Celestial Bonds

In the night, stars align,
Whispers echo, hearts entwine.
Galaxies dance, a sight so grand,
Together we traverse this land.

Moonlight guides our quiet path,
Infinite love, a gentle math.
Souls connected, a cosmic thread,
In every moment, joy is spread.

Our Harmonious Expedition

With every step, our hearts sing,
A melody of love we bring.
Through valleys deep and mountains high,
Together, we shall touch the sky.

Hand in hand, we face the storms,
In each other's arms, we find our forms.
Chasing sunrises, breathing free,
In this journey, just you and me.

Finding Home in Each Other

In a world of chaos, we found grace,
A peaceful haven, a warm embrace.
Within your eyes, I see my place,
Together, we create our space.

Every moment shared feels right,
Guided by love's gentle light.
Through trials faced and laughter shared,
In your heart, I'm never scared.

Unveiling the Blissful Expedition

With each dawn, fresh tales to weave,
In this journey, we truly believe.
Mountains of joy and rivers of dreams,
Threads of fate, unraveling seams.

As we wander, hands intertwined,
Discovering treasures, love defined.
Laughter echoes, a sweet serenade,
Through every twist, our bond won't fade.

Armed with Love's Compass

In the depths of our hearts, we find the way,
With every beat, love leads us to stay.
Through storms and trials, we hold it tight,
Guided by passion, we chase the light.

With whispers of dreams, we chart the course,
In the strength of our bond, we gather force.
Every challenge met, we conquer as one,
Armed with love's compass, our journey's begun.

The stars up above, they twinkle and gleam,
Encouraging us to follow the dream.
Hand in hand we tread on, no fear in sight,
With love's compass guiding, we embrace the night.

Mosaic of Togetherness

Each moment we share, a tile in the scheme,
Crafting our lives like a beautiful dream.
Colors so vibrant, reflecting our trust,
In unity's bond, our love is a must.

With laughter and joy, we blend every hue,
A masterpiece formed, just me and you.
Through trials we face, our pieces align,
In this mosaic dear, our lives intertwine.

Through seasons of change, our patterns will grow,
Intertwined stories, the love we will show.
Together we stand, through thick and through thin,
Creating a legacy, together we win.

Summit of Trust

As we climb higher, the path may be steep,
But hand in hand, our promises we keep.
With every step forward, we build the way,
At the summit of trust, forever we'll stay.

Embracing our hopes, we rise with the sun,
In the warmth of our bond, two hearts become one.
With every breath taken, we find our embrace,
In this sacred journey, we cherish the space.

The view from the top, a sight to behold,
With faith as our guide, our story unfolds.
Together we've conquered, together we soar,
At the summit of trust, we'll always want more.

A Radiant Fusion

When our souls entwine, a spark ignites,
In a dance of passion, we reach new heights.
A radiant fusion, our energies blend,
In this cosmic rhythm, there's no end.

With colors that shimmer, we paint the skies,
Together we shine, love never lies.
In the glow of each moment, we find our way,
In this radiant fusion, forever we'll stay.

As stars collide, they create a new light,
In the warmth of our love, we banish the night.
Two hearts, one vision, our dreams intertwine,
In this timeless dance, our spirits align.

Love's Lantern in the Dark

In shadows deep where silence dwells,
A flicker glows, a tale it tells.
A beacon bright through endless night,
Love's lantern shines, a guiding light.

It dances softly on the walls,
Echoing sweetly, love enthralls.
Each whispered word, a gentle spark,
That ignites hope within the dark.

Through trials faced and fears we bear,
Hand in hand, we find our prayer.
With every beat, our hearts align,
In every pulse, a love divine.

Together we forge a brighter way,
As night retreats to greet the day.
With courage born from trust so true,
Love's lantern leads, forever new.

Cherished Steps Side by Side

Through winding paths, we walk as one,
Each step we take, a race well-run.
In laughter shared and silence sweet,
Cherished moments, our hearts greet.

With fingers laced, we brave the storm,
In every touch, our spirits warm.
Together strong, we face the tide,
With every stride, love's joy our guide.

In gardens lush where blossoms bloom,
We dance together, chasing gloom.
With whispered dreams that softly glide,
Our hopes alight, side by side.

Through every trial, hand in hand,
In freedom's song, together stand.
The world may shift, but our embrace,
Is where we'll find our sacred space.

Beyond the Horizon of Us

In twilight's glow, the world unfolds,
A promise whispered, dreams untold.
Beyond the edge where skies meet sea,
Lives the realm where hearts run free.

With every dawn, a blush of light,
A canvas painted, pure and bright.
We chase the sun, our spirits high,
Together bound, we soar the sky.

Through valleys deep and mountains wide,
In each adventure, love's our guide.
No limit found, no edge to fear,
Beyond the horizon, we draw near.

In every moment, time stands still,
The vast expanse bends to our will.
In this journey, hearts entwine,
Beyond the horizon, love is thine.

The Breath of Union

In mirrored souls where silence plays,
The breath of union softly sways.
With shared exhales, we find our place,
In every heartbeat, an endless grace.

Two worlds converge in whispered dreams,
Bound by the flow of gentle streams.
With eyes that shine, a knowing glance,
In love's embrace, we take our chance.

With every sigh, we weave the night,
In every laugh, the dawn's delight.
Together we write a song so true,
The breath of union, me and you.

Through trials faced and joys intricate,
Our spirits dance, we resonate.
In cherished moments, we find our song,
In love's sweet breath, we all belong.

Celebrations in Togetherness

In laughter we unite,
Hearts beat in delight.
Under twinkling skies,
Friendship never dies.

With every joyful cheer,
We draw our loved ones near.
Together we will shine,
In moments pure, divine.

In the warmth of the night,
We dance in shared light.
Every hug a treasure,
A bond beyond measure.

The music fills the air,
Life's burdens we do share.
As candles softly glow,
Grateful hearts overflow.

Through seasons we will roam,
Together, we find home.
In times of joy and pain,
Our love will ever reign.

A Dance Among the Stars

Beneath the velvet sky,
We twirl, my love and I.
With stardust in our hair,
A cosmic dream we share.

Galaxies spinning bright,
Holding on through the night.
In each other's embrace,
We find our sacred space.

Moonlight casts a glow,
With every step, we flow.
Time seems to stand still,
As we dance at will.

With every whispered sigh,
The universe is nigh.
Cosmic rhythms we trace,
In this endless place.

Together hand in hand,
In this enchanted land.
Among the stars we play,
In love, we drift away.

The Joy Within the Journey

Every step we shall take,
New memories we make.
With laughter as our guide,
In love we shall abide.

Through mountains high and low,
In sun and in the snow.
Finding beauty in strife,
This journey is our life.

With open hearts we roam,
Every corner feels like home.
In the trials we discover,
The strength we find in each other.

As rivers flow and bend,
Our spirits seldom end.
In the tales that we weave,
There's joy in what we believe.

Together we shall soar,
Through every distant shore.
In the joy we uncover,
Life's true gift is each other.

Threads of Forever

Woven in every thread,
Stories softly said.
In the fabric of time,
We find our perfect rhyme.

Each stitch is a memory,
A glimpse of what will be.
Binding us ever tight,
In shadows and in light.

Colors blend and swirl,
Life's tapestry unfurl.
Through laughter, through tears,
We mend our hopes and fears.

In the loom of the heart,
No distance keeps us apart.
With threads both strong and fine,
We craft our sacred line.

Eternity unfolds,
In the warmth, we hold.
Together we create,
A bond that won't abate.

Oasis of Serenity

In the stillness, waters gleam,
Whispers of peace, like gentle dreams.
Palm trees sway in soft embrace,
A tranquil heart finds its place.

Sunset paints the sky in gold,
All worries fade, the night unfolds.
Stars emerge in the calming haze,
In this moment, my spirit plays.

Waves of solace kiss the shore,
A secret world I can't ignore.
Nature's song, a sweet refrain,
In this oasis, I feel no pain.

Breath of earth, a soothing balm,
In your beauty, I find my calm.
Time stands still, as shadows dance,
In this haven, I take a chance.

Gathering Sparks of Joy

In laughter's glow, we gather round,
Friendships bloom in love profound.
Every smile, a light we share,
In our hearts, joy fills the air.

Moments cherished, bright as day,
In simple acts, we find our way.
Stories woven, the past alive,
With every hug, our spirits thrive.

Dancing shadows, echoes bright,
Under stars, we own the night.
Hope ignites in every glance,
Life unfolds, an endless dance.

Together we dream, reach for more,
Building castles on distant shore.
In this circle, love won't fade,
Sparks of joy will never trade.

Chasing the Sunlight

Morning whispers, a brand new day,
Chasing shadows, I find my way.
Golden rays break through the mist,
Each fleeting moment, I can't resist.

Wandering fields where wildflowers sigh,
In every bloom, a reason to try.
Under the sun's warm, gentle light,
Hope ignites and takes to flight.

With open arms, I greet the dawn,
Letting go of what's withdrawn.
Down the paths that nature shows,
In the sunlight, my spirit grows.

Every twinkle, a promise bright,
In the chase, I find my flight.
Embracing all that life can give,
In this warmth, I truly live.

The Colors of Connection

Brush strokes blend in vibrant hues,
In every shade, a different muse.
Hands entwined, our stories flow,
Through colors deep, our spirits glow.

In shared laughter, we paint the sky,
Building bridges as moments fly.
Harmony found in each embrace,
In this tapestry, we find our place.

Silent whispers in the night,
The bond we share, pure delight.
Through every tear and every smile,
In vibrant tones, we walk each mile.

Cascading shades of love and care,
A gallery hung in the open air.
Together, we weave the threads of time,
In the colors of connection, we climb.

Sunflowers in Winter

Golden faces in the frost,
Stand tall against the freeze,
With petals crisped by cold,
They whisper tales of ease.

Beneath the grayish skies,
They reach for distant light,
With dreams of warmer days,
In the depths of the night.

Snowflakes dance around them,
Like stars against the earth,
Each bloom a silent promise,
Of spring's joyful rebirth.

Their roots hold firm in silence,
While seasons turn and sway,
A testament to courage,
In the depths of decay.

When winter's grip is strong,
And hope seems far away,
These sunflowers stand defiant,
A bright and bold array.

The Light After the Mist

In shadows where doubts linger,
The fog begins to part,
A glimmer beckons softly,
It warms the quiet heart.

Whispers of the dawn break,
As thoughts begin to clear,
Each step a little lighter,
Chasing away the fear.

Beyond the shifting veils,
New colors start to bloom,
Emerging from the silence,
Life casts away the gloom.

As rays of gold burst forth,
They paint the world anew,
With every trace of mist,
A brighter path comes through.

So trust the light that's coming,
Let hope forever last,
For every dawn is waiting,
To chase away the past.

A Symphony of Two

When notes entwine like lovers,
A melody takes flight,
With rhythms softly pulsing,
Through the quiet night.

Each whisper of the strings,
A warmth that fills the air,
Their harmony a beacon,
In moments rich and rare.

A dance of sweet emotions,
That only they can know,
In every chord's embrace,
Love's tender ebb and flow.

From silence grows the music,
A language pure and true,
In the symphony of two,
Where hearts and hopes renew.

Together they create worlds,
With every single note,
A timeless serenade,
In which their spirits float.

Anchored Hearts

In storms that rage like oceans,
Two souls find solid ground,
With roots that dig much deeper,
They're bound where love is found.

Through waves of doubt and fear,
They hold through darkest nights,
Their anchor forged in trust,
A bond that ignites lights.

With every push and pull,
Together they will rise,
Their hearts a steady compass,
Guided by shared skies.

No winds will break their promise,
No tide will tear apart,
The anchors of their longing,
That bind each loving heart.

In gentle lull and fury,
They'll navigate the sea,
With anchored hearts united,
In love's vast harmony.

The Bridge of Affection

Across the river, hearts align,
A path that shines through every storm.
With gentle whispers, love entwines,
In soft embraces, spirits warm.

Beneath the arch of dreams we share,
We walk with trust, side by side.
No weight of worry, no need for care,
In this connection, we confide.

The bridge stands strong, though time may wane,
Each step we take is worth the while.
Through every joy, through every pain,
We build a future with our smile.

So let us tread on sacred ground,
With every heartbeat shared in grace.
In every silence, love is found,
In every glance, our rightful place.

Together still, as seasons change,
Our love, a flow that knows no end.
Through every challenge, we'll rearrange,
On this bridge, my love, my friend.

Navigating Stars

In the velvet night, we find our way,
Guided by constellations bright.
With every wish that we convey,
The cosmos whispers, stars ignite.

Each twinkle speaks of dreams yet seen,
A promise held in endless space.
With you beside me, I feel serene,
Through the vast universe, we trace.

The Milky Way, our compass true,
With laughter echoing through the void.
Hand in hand, with skies of blue,
We'll dance where hopes and dreams are buoyed.

Eclipses may come, shadows may fall,
Yet love remains our shining light.
In galaxies where we stand tall,
We navigate through darkest night.

So let us soar on wings of grace,
A journey bound by open hearts.
Together, here in time and space,
We weave our destiny, our arts.

Hand in Hand Through the Fog

As morning breaks, the mist does rise,
We walk the path where shadows play.
With trust in you, my heart complies,
Together, we'll find our way.

In whispered stories, secrets soar,
Each step a promise, firm and bright.
With every heartbeat, I want more,
Through veils of grey, we chase the light.

The fog may wrap, the world may blur,
But side by side, we'll face the day.
In silence shared, the heart will stir,
In your embrace, I wish to stay.

Through twists and turns, our spirits blend,
With courage found in love's soft glow.
No fear can break, no time can bend,
For hand in hand, we surely know.

So let us forge our destiny,
With every stride, we'll write our song.
In this adventure, you and me,
Hand in hand, we will be strong.

Embracing Each Tomorrow

With dawn's first light, a canvas bare,
We paint our hopes in shades of gold.
In every moment, love lays there,
A treasure chest with stories told.

Through gentle laughter, dreams we weave,
Boundless visions that stretch and rise.
With open hearts, we dare believe,
In every loss, there is a prize.

Embracing shadows, finding grace,
With you, I walk this winding road.
Together, we create our space,
A bond that lightens every load.

In future's arms, we trust and grow,
With every heartbeat, we ignite.
Through trials faced and joys in tow,
We carve our path, our spirits bright.

So here we stand, together strong,
In unity, we shape tomorrow.
When storms may come, we'll sing our song,
Embracing laughter, love, and sorrow.

The Colors of Conjoined Hearts

In whispers sweet, our colors blend,
Two souls unite, on paths they wend.
Threads of laughter, hues of trust,
Together we shine, in love we must.

Through storms and sun, we paint the sky,
With every heartbeat, love won't die.
Crimson dreams, and azure sighs,
In the canvas of us, beauty lies.

Golden moments, soft and rare,
Pastel hopes float in the air.
Each shade tells tales of joy and pain,
In our joined hearts, love will reign.

Emerald nights, where secrets flow,
Violet memories begin to grow.
Colorful futures beckon near,
With every brushstroke, we draw cheer.

Together we'll dance, a radiant spark,
In a gallery bright, forever marked.
A masterpiece born from the start,
The colors of conjoined hearts.

Unraveling Love's Tapestry

In threads of gold, stories entwine,
A rich tapestry, yours and mine.
Every stitch a moment spent,
A journey crafted, love's intent.

The patterns weave both joy and strife,
Through vibrant colors, we find life.
Each knot a problem we mend,
A fabric strong, that won't bend.

In shadows cast, the light will break,
We gather strength from each heartache.
As needle glides through fabric thick,
We stitch together love's magic.

Unraveling tales of laughter shared,
Embroidered dreams, how much we cared.
With every thread, a memory grows,
Through life's loom, our love bestows.

In the grand design, we find our place,
Stitching the moments, in time and space.
A tapestry woven, rich and vast,
Unraveling love, forever clasped.

A Symphony of Vows

In quiet whispers, vows arise,
A symphony beneath the skies.
Each note a promise, sweet and true,
In harmony, I stand with you.

Through ups and downs, our song does play,
A melody that guides our way.
In every chord, a love so pure,
With every beat, we can endure.

The rhythm of our hearts entwined,
In perfect sync, our fates aligned.
Together we dance, a waltz divine,
In this symphony, forever shine.

With every measure, love's refrain,
Is written in joy, and even pain.
The echoes linger, soft and clear,
In symphonic vows, forever near.

So let us play this song of ours,
Among the stars, and blooming flowers.
A symphony of love's true story,
In every note, resounding glory.

Charting Our Love Story

In ink of hope, our tale begins,
A map of dreams, where love now spins.
Each page a moment, joyfully penned,
In the book of us, our hearts blend.

With compass set, we navigate,
Through winding paths we'll celebrate.
A journey shared, through thick and thin,
With every chapter, new life within.

The mountains high, the valleys deep,
Together we find, the love we keep.
Through storms and stars, we write our fate,
In every word, we gravitate.

Each sunset paints our stories bright,
As stars align in the velvet night.
Turning pages of laughter and tears,
Charting our love through all the years.

In every verse, our passions soar,
In the story of us, we'll explore.
Forever bound, on this journey free,
Our love story, just you and me.

A Garden of Shared Seasons

In spring we bloom, soft and bright,
Colors dance in morning light.
The fragrance sweet, our laughter shared,
In this calm space, we are prepared.

Summer brings the sun's warm glow,
Together we watch the rivers flow.
Underneath the shady trees,
Whispers carried by the breeze.

As autumn leaves begin to fall,
We gather close, embracing all.
The golden hues paint the ground,
In every corner, love is found.

Winter's chill wraps us tight,
Yet hearts are warm, our spirits light.
By the fire, stories unfold,
In the quiet, our love is bold.

Each season's gift, a treasure rare,
In our garden, beyond compare.
With time we'll tend, grow and mend,
In every moment, love will blend.

Flowing Rivers of Trust

Beneath the surface, waters flow,
Secrets kept, only we know.
With every ripple, promises made,
In this bond, our fears will fade.

Through winding paths, the river glides,
Along its banks, our hearts confide.
In gentle currents, we find our way,
Together navigating each new day.

The gentle splash of truth is clear,
In each reflection, you are near.
We navigate both calm and storm,
In every twist, our hearts stay warm.

As we drift through time's embrace,
You are my anchor, my sacred space.
With trust as deep as oceans wide,
Together, we will always ride.

These flowing rivers, pure and free,
Join our souls in harmony.
In every turn, we find our grace,
Our bond, a journey we embrace.

Serenading Each Other's Souls

In twilight's glow, our voices blend,
Soft melodies, as we transcend.
Each note a whisper, a gentle sigh,
In this moment, together we fly.

With every strum of the guitar,
Echoes of love from near and far.
The moonlight dances on your face,
In this serenade, we find our place.

Our laughter mingles with the song,
In perfect rhythm, we belong.
Each verse we share brings us near,
In harmony, we have no fear.

Every heartbeat sings your name,
In this duet, we're both aflame.
As starlit skies bear witness true,
Our souls entwined, forever new.

A serenade that never ends,
A love that grows, our spirits mend.
In every chord, our truth we find,
In this enactment, hearts aligned.

The Map of Our Hearts

In quiet corners, secrets dwell,
With ink and dreams, we weave our spell.
Through tangled paths, we trace the part,
Creating gently the map of our heart.

Every mark tells a story of old,
Of journeys taken, both brave and bold.
Each memory drawn with a tender touch,
In the vast wilderness, we seek so much.

Mountains high and valleys low,
In every challenge, our love will grow.
Binding threads of hope and grace,
Together we navigate this space.

Through stormy skies and sunny days,
Our map unfolds in myriad ways.
With compass true, we chart our course,
In every moment, love's gentle force.

With every twist, a new surprise,
The map of our hearts never lies.
Together we travel, hand in hand,
In this grand journey, we make our stand.

Together We Rise

In the dawn's soft glow, we stand tall,
Hand in hand, we face it all.
With every challenge, we unite,
Together we rise, hearts alight.

Through storms that rage, we find our spark,
Guiding each other out of the dark.
With voices raised, we forge ahead,
Together in dreams, no words left unsaid.

In laughter shared and tears that flow,
We build a bond that continues to grow.
Every hurdle, we gracefully climb,
Together in rhythm, in our own time.

Through valleys deep and peaks so high,
With wings of hope, we learn to fly.
In the tapestry of life, we weave,
Together we rise, we truly believe.

Echoes of Sweet Nothings

In whispered dreams under the moon,
Your voice a soft, enchanting tune.
With every secret shared in the night,
Echoes of sweet nothings take flight.

In the quiet moments, hearts align,
Lost in a gaze, our souls intertwine.
Words unspoken hang in the air,
Echoes of sweet love, beyond compare.

Through delicate laughter, time stands still,
In the warmth of your touch, I feel the thrill.
With sweet serenades, we dance so free,
Echoes of sweet nothings, just you and me.

In dreams we wander, hand in hand,
Building a world, so gently planned.
With every heartbeat, love's gentle call,
Echoes of sweet nothings, that bind us all.

The Firefly Nights

Under stars that shimmer bright,
We chase the dreams in shallow light.
With fireflies dancing, a nightly show,
In the magic of dusk, our hopes will grow.

In the whispers of the gentle breeze,
We find our freedom among the trees.
With laughter twinkling like the stars' delight,
We embrace the warmth of the firefly night.

Hidden treasures in a jar we keep,
Moments like these, forever deep.
As the world sleeps, our hearts ignite,
In the embrace of the firefly night.

With every glow, a promise made,
Together forever, we won't be swayed.
In these fleeting hours, love takes flight,
In the heart of the firefly night.

Dreams in Tandem

We weave our dreams, hand in hand,
In worlds where wishes softly land.
With every heartbeat, our visions blend,
Dreams in tandem, no need to pretend.

With stars as guides, we tread the skies,
Exploring horizons, where adventure lies.
In laughter shared, we chase the sun,
Dreams in tandem, two hearts as one.

Through valleys of hope, we find a way,
In the palette of life, we paint our day.
With colors bright, we face the unknown,
Dreams in tandem, together we've grown.

In every step, we leave a mark,
Two vibrant souls igniting the spark.
As shadows fade, our spirits rise,
Dreams in tandem, beneath the skies.

The Melody of Us

In twilight's glow, we dance and sway,
Every note, a word we say.
The rhythm wraps, so warm and tight,
Together in this sweet twilight.

Through laughter shared, our spirits rise,
Like stars that light the evening skies.
A harmony that knows no end,
In every heartbeat, love we send.

With whispers soft, our secrets blend,
The chorus echoes, hearts transcend.
In this embrace, the world feels new,
A symphony composed for two.

As time unfolds, our melody flows,
A timeless tale that always grows.
For in each note, the memories rest,
In love's sweet song, we are so blessed.

Roots of Joy

In gardens bright, where laughter thrives,
The roots of joy begin our lives.
Amidst the blooms, our spirits soar,
Each petal whispers, "Love's encore."

The sun's embrace warms every day,
Through storms and clouds, we find our way.
With every step, we plant our dreams,
In fields of hope, where sunlight gleams.

From tiny seeds, adventures grow,
In every heartbeat, love's warm glow.
As branches stretch, our hearts unite,
In this bright world, we find our light.

Through changing seasons, hand in hand,
Together strong, our dreams we stand.
In roots of joy, we find our grace,
A timeless dance, in warm embrace.

Mosaics of Memories

Each shard of time, a story told,
In vibrant hues, our lives unfold.
With laughter bright, or tears that flow,
We craft our dreams, let love bestow.

Through glimpses caught in golden frames,
We cherish moments, keep their names.
From whispered tales of days gone by,
To future dreams that touch the sky.

Mosaics built with threads of care,
Connect our hearts, a bond to share.
In every piece, a spark ignites,
A dance of joy in starry nights.

With every breath, we weave and spin,
In each embrace, the warmth within.
Together wrapped in colors bold,
Our tapestry of life unfolds.

The Unwritten Story

In pages blank, the tale awaits,
A journey drawn by love and fate.
With every step on paths unknown,
A canvas vast, our hearts have grown.

In whispered hopes, our dreams ignite,
As shadows dance in soft moonlight.
With every pause, new chapters start,
In ink of love, we write our art.

Through laughter's echo, tears we share,
A winding road that leads us there.
In every twist, a truth unveiled,
Together bound, we can't be failed.

Each heartbeat writes a line so true,
An endless tale for me and you.
With every dawn, the story grows,
An unwritten dream, our love bestows.

Unveiling New Horizons

Beyond the mountains, skies unfold,
Whispers of dreams in colors bold.
Every step, a story told,
In the light of futures gold.

Waves of hope crash on the shore,
Echoes of what we're longing for.
Embrace the change, seek to explore,
There's so much more than ever before.

Through the valleys, shadows play,
Guiding us along the way.
In the dance of night and day,
New paths await, come what may.

With open hearts, we cast our gaze,
To the heights of brighter days.
Each moment's spark, a gentle blaze,
In this life, joy only stays.

Together we rise, hand in hand,
Transforming dreams into a land.
With courage strong, together stand,
A world anew, our hearts expand.

Cultivating Shared Joy

In laughter shared, our spirits bloom,
Soft melodies chase away the gloom.
Each smile a flower, fragrance sweet,
Together we make our lives complete.

With every moment, hearts entwine,
We weave our stories, yours and mine.
In the warmth of friendship's glow,
A tapestry of love will grow.

Kind words like raindrops softly fall,
Nurturing bonds that bind us all.
In every hug, a sacred space,
Creating joy, our saving grace.

Through the trials, hand in hand,
Together we will always stand.
With open arms, we take the leap,
Finding joy in what we keep.

So let us dance beneath the stars,
Celebrate our dreams, our scars.
In the symphony of life's embrace,
We cultivate shared joy and grace.

Embracing All That Is Us

In the mirror, reflections blend,
All our stories, we comprehend.
With every flaw, a beauty shines,
Embracing hearts, where love aligns.

In laughter's echo, we unite,
Shadows fade in love's warm light.
Together we face the storms that rage,
Turning each chapter, we turn the page.

Through differences, we find our thread,
A vibrant tapestry, brightly spread.
In every tear, a lesson learned,
With open hearts, our fires burned.

Let our voices rise like the dawn,
In harmony, we carry on.
Celebrating all that makes us whole,
Embracing the depths of every soul.

In this journey, hand in hand,
With love as our unbreakable strand.
Together, we blossom and trust,
In the beauty of all that is us.

Through the Seasons of Us

In spring's embrace, we start anew,
With blooms so bright and skies so blue.
Each moment shared, a budding dream,
Together, life, a flowing stream.

As summer sings with joyful light,
Our laughter dances, hearts take flight.
With endless days beneath the sun,
In every heartbeat, we are one.

Autumn whispers with a golden hue,
Leaves falling softly, aged and true.
We gather warmth, a cloak of love,
Together we soar, like the dove.

In winter's chill, we hold each other,
A fire warms, like no other.
Through storms we stand, our spirits high,
In every tear, a shared sigh.

Through seasons' change, our bond will grow,
In every heartbeat, love will flow.
A canvas bright, our story spun,
In life's embrace, we are as one.

Portraits of Joyful Union

In frames adorned with memories sweet,
We gather moments, the heart's own beat.
Each snapshot glows with love's embrace,
A tapestry of time and space.

Laughing faces in sunlight's glow,
Captured joy in the ebb and flow.
Together we stand, forever bold,
In portraits rich, our tales unfold.

In whispered dreams and quiet nights,
We savor days, our shared delights.
A brush of hands, a loving glance,
In every glance, a sweet romance.

As seasons turn and shadows play,
Our union thrives in night and day.
With every smile, our spirits sing,
A joyful bond, our hearts take wing.

Through frames adorned, our love will shine,
A picture perfect, yours and mine.
In every stroke, in every hue,
A portrait bright of me and you.

Harbors of Heartfelt Commitment

In quiet bays where dreams align,
We anchor hearts, your hand in mine.
With steadfast love, we brave the tide,
In every storm, we will abide.

The lighthouse beams, a guiding light,
Through darkest nights, love keeps us bright.
In every wave, our promise stands,
Together strong, two drifting sands.

With every breath, we cross the sea,
In harbors warm, just you and me.
An anchored soul, forever tied,
In every pulse, our love will bide.

So let the winds of fortune blow,
In all we face, our love will grow.
Harbors safe in life's vast quest,
With you, my heart finds gentle rest.

Through every tide, our dreams will sway,
In deepest depths, we find our way.
A soulful bond, a strong duet,
In every moment, no regret.

Through the Lens of Togetherness

With lenses wide, we capture light,
Every glance, a spark so bright.
Through photos shared, our truths unfold,
In every image, hearts made bold.

Each snapshot tells a timeless tale,
Of whispered dreams where lovers sail.
Through laughter shared and tears we've shed,
Our journey marked in patterns spread.

In frames of joy, we find our place,
In candid smiles, a warm embrace.
With every click, love's moment seized,
Through every shot, our hearts appeased.

As time moves on, we still remain,
In every frame, love's sweet refrain.
Through the lens, the world we see,
In unity, just you and me.

Together always, hand in hand,
Captured memories, forever stand.
Through every picture, love's bright art,
In every image, one beating heart.

Love Letters to the Future

In dreams we write our hopes in ink,
A world awaits, more than we think.
With every stroke, a wish to soar,
To find a path, to open doors.

In time we'll cherish all we've penned,
Connections deep that never end.
Each word a promise, softly sealed,
With hearts aflame, all love revealed.

The pages turn, our story grows,
Through storms and sun, the river flows.
We send our letters, brave and true,
With every wish, we dream anew.

A thousand futures in our hands,
We build with care, we make our plans.
Hand in hand, we face the light,
In love's embrace, our hearts take flight.

Adventures in Bloom

In fields where wildflowers dance and sway,
We find the joy in bright array.
With laughter, we embrace the day,
Each petal whispers, come and play.

Beneath the sky, so vast and blue,
We wander paths where dreams come true.
The scent of earth, the sun's warm kiss,
In every moment, perfect bliss.

With every step, the world unfolds,
New stories waiting to be told.
We chase the breeze and breathe the air,
In nature's arms, without a care.

Let's dance among the blooms so bright,
In vibrant colors, pure delight.
Adventures call us, wild and free,
With hearts so light, just you and me.

A Fiesta of Hearts

Beneath the stars, we gather near,
With laughter, love, and endless cheer.
In vibrant colors, life's a dance,
A fiesta where we take our chance.

With every beat, our spirits rise,
In joyous moments, truth belies.
We raise our glasses, voices blend,
Together now, the night won't end.

The music swells, our souls ignite,
In every step, we find the light.
A celebration, warm and grand,
In unity, together we stand.

From heart to heart, we share the love,
As stars twinkle bright high above.
In this fiesta, dreams take flight,
A tapestry of pure delight.

Whispers of the Wind

In gentle breezes, secrets flow,
Tales of the past, the future glow.
The whispers call, they speak so clear,
With every sigh, the world draws near.

Through rustling leaves, the stories weave,
In nature's arms, we humbly believe.
The wind carries dreams across the skies,
A melody where silence lies.

With open hearts, we listen close,
In every gust, we find our prose.
The echoes of time, they softly play,
Guiding us gently on our way.

So let us wander with the breeze,
In whispered tones, we find our ease.
For every moment, sweet and kind,
Is wrapped in whispers of the wind.

Seasons of Together

In spring's embrace, we bloom anew,
Fresh scents of life, a vibrant hue.
Through summer's warmth, hand in hand,
We dance with joy across the land.

As autumn leaves begin to fall,
Whispers of change, we heed the call.
In winter's chill, we find our fire,
A tapestry of love's desire.

Through seasons shifting, hearts entwine,
In every phase, a love divine.
Together woven, strong and true,
Our journey's thread, forever new.

Each moment cherished, time stands still,
Together facing all we will.
From dawn to dusk, through joy and strife,
Each season shared, a gift of life.

Radiant Tomorrows

In dawn's soft light, our dreams take flight,
With every hope, we chase the bright.
Together we embrace the dawn,
A canvas vast, where love is drawn.

With starlit skies, we weave our fate,
A tapestry that won't abate.
Hand in hand, we face the dawn,
With radiant tomorrows, we're reborn.

Each heartbeat whispers, 'Here we stand,'
In unity, we break the sand.
Through shadows cast, our hearts ignite,
In every challenge, we find light.

Together we will chase the stars,
Defy the odds, erase the scars.
In future's glow, we'll find our way,
Radiant tomorrows, come what may.

Love's Gentle Uprising

In quiet moments, hearts may sway,
A gentle tug, a soft array.
Through whispered words and tender glances,
Love's gentle uprising, sweet romances.

As moonlight spills on silken sheets,
Two souls in harmony, love repeats.
With tender hands and eyes that gleam,
We nurture hopes, we build our dream.

In everyday, small acts arise,
A warm embrace, two longing sighs.
Through trials faced, our spirits soar,
Love's gentle uprising, we explore.

In laughter shared, and tears that flow,
Together, still, our feelings grow.
With every heartbeat, love's refrain,
An uprising sweet, a joyous gain.

The Rhythm of Belonging

In every heartbeat, a rhythm found,
A pulse of love, a soothing sound.
With every step upon the ground,
The melody of belonging, profound.

Through laughter bright, and sorrows shared,
In all the moments, we've truly cared.
Each voice a note in harmony,
Together, crafting our symphony.

In shadows cast, we find our light,
A dance together, spirits bright.
The rhythm beats, our hearts align,
In every glance, our souls entwine.

As seasons change and time moves on,
The melody of love's sweet song.
In every chapter, holding strong,
We write the verses of belonging.

Beyond the Horizon of Togetherness

We stand hand in hand, side by side,
With dreams that soar, like birds on a glide.
Through valleys of hope and mountains high,
Together we reach for the endless sky.

In whispers of dawn, our hearts intertwine,
Each moment we share, so tender, divine.
With every sunset, new colors unfold,
A tapestry woven, more precious than gold.

Beyond every challenge, through storm and rain,
We find our peace, where love will remain.
A journey unbroken, our souls in a dance,
In the light of togetherness, we take each chance.

Through laughter and tears, we cherish the ride,
In the warmth of your gaze, I take so much pride.
With every heartbeat, our stories align,
Beyond the horizon, forever you're mine.

Echoes of Laughter and Love

In a room filled with joy, laughter rings bright,
Memories blend in the soft evening light.
Each chuckle a verse, a sweet song we sing,
Echoes of moments together, take wing.

With each playful glance, our spirits take flight,
In stories retold, our hearts feel so light.
A tapestry woven with threads of delight,
Frame by frame captured in love's gentle light.

Together we dance on the stage of our dreams,
With giggles and whispers, together we beam.
In the symphony of us, a rhapsody flows,
Echoes of laughter remain as it grows.

Through whispers and sighs, we forge our own beat,
In the comfort of arms, our world feels complete.
With every heartbeat, a promise we make,
Tomorrow awaits, together we wake.

Candlelight Promises

In the glow of the flame, our secrets unfold,
Whispers of dreams more precious than gold.
Two shadows entwined in a soft, tender light,
Candlelight promises kept through the night.

With flickering warmth, our hearts learn to dance,
In moments of silence, we revel in chance.
Each flicker a vow that the night will embrace,
In the cradle of love, a timeless place.

Under the stars, with our hands tightly clasped,
In the beauty of stillness, our futures are grasped.
With whispers and laughter, the night stretches long,
Candlelight promises sing our love song.

Through shadows of doubt, we find our own way,
A flicker of hope, brighter each day.
With every heartbeat, as candles may flick,
Our love is the fire, forever to stick.

Pathways of Love

Through winding trails where our footsteps trace,
Each path held with care, a gentle embrace.
With every step forward, love leads us along,
Together we journey, where we both belong.

In the garden of memories, blossoms arise,
Tales of our laughter under wide-open skies.
We follow the stars that illuminate night,
Creating a map where our hearts feel the light.

Through valleys of struggle, we rise side by side,
In the strength of our bond, we have nothing to hide.
With whispers of hope, we paint out the scene,
Among paths of love, our spirits convene.

In the rhythm of life, each heartbeat's a guide,
Through pathways of love, forever we stride.
Together we wander, our souls intertwined,
In the magic of love, true happiness find.

The Bridge of Forever

With gentle steps we tread the path,
A bridge of whispers, love's sweet wrath.
Above the river, time stands still,
Where hearts entwine, and dreams fulfill.

Beneath the stars, our laughter rings,
Each secret share, the joy it brings.
Together we walk, side by side,
On this bridge, where hopes abide.

In every moment, memories flow,
As colors dance in twilight's glow.
Each heartbeat echoes like a song,
In this sacred space, where we belong.

Through storms and sun, we find our way,
With every dawn, a brand new day.
The bridge of forever, strong and true,
In every step, I walk with you.

Bound by the love that knows no end,
Through every turn, around each bend.
Together we'll face what lies ahead,
On the bridge of dreams, our spirits fed.

Echoes of a Shared Dream

In twilight's hush, the whispers rise,
Echoes dance beneath the skies.
A shared dream bright, it calls our name,
In every heart, a flickering flame.

We weave our wishes with silken thread,
In the tapestry of words unsaid.
Together we soar on feathered wings,
In the space where hope forever clings.

Through valleys deep and mountains high,
Our laughter echoes, a sweet reply.
In every shadow, light shall gleam,
For we are bound by a shared dream.

With every heartbeat, the world aligns,
Together we write our own designs.
In the silence, our spirits beam,
United forever, in this shared dream.

As stars align to light the night,
We'll chase the dawn, in pure delight.
In the depths of our souls, we'll know,
The echoes of dreams that forever glow.

Starlit Promises

Underneath a blanket of stars,
We whisper secrets from afar.
With promise etched in night's embrace,
A dance of hope, a sacred space.

Each twinkle holds a tale we weave,
In constellations, we believe.
With every wish upon a light,
Our starlit vows shall guide the night.

As comets blaze across the sky,
So do our hearts, unbound, fly high.
Together, we'll write our own fate,
In the glow of love, we celebrate.

With every heartbeat, dreams ignite,
In the quiet, we find our might.
Starlit promises, a bond so fair,
In every moment, love laid bare.

The cosmos knows our every thought,
The battles fought and lessons taught.
In the night's embrace, we shine so bright,
Together forever, in endless light.

Embracing the Horizon

As dawn unfolds with golden hue,
We stand as one, me and you.
With arms wide open to the day,
Embracing all that comes our way.

The horizon calls, a promise new,
Where dreams unfold in vibrant view.
Together we chase the morning light,
Hand in hand, hearts bold and bright.

Through fields of hope and skies so wide,
We'll find our path, our hearts our guide.
In every step, we'll forge our tale,
As waves of time whisper and sail.

With every sunrise, a chance reborn,
In love's embrace, we'll weather the storm.
Together we'll dance on life's vast stage,
Embracing the horizon, turning the page.

As twilight falls and stars appear,
We'll cherish moments we hold dear.
In every heartbeat, love's refrain,
Together we'll rise again, again.

Beneath the Canopy of Trust

In shadows where whispers play,
Hearts entwined, we find our way.
Leaves above, they rustle low,
Promises in breezes flow.

With every tear that softly falls,
We gather strength, heed nature's calls.
Roots that bind, so deep, so true,
In this haven, I trust you.

Sunlight dapples on our skin,
In this space, we both begin.
Together here, we dance and twirl,
Beneath the leaves, our dreams unfurl.

The sky, a canvas, vast and wide,
In unity, we stand with pride.
Each gentle breeze a soft caress,
Beneath this canopy, we are blessed.

Through seasons change, we hold on tight,
In darkness, find our source of light.
Hand in hand, we'll face the storm,
In trust, our spirits stay warm.

A Map to Endless Laughter

On pathways paved with giggles bright,
We wander free in pure delight.
With every step, a joke unfolds,
A treasure map of joy and gold.

Across the hills where laughter gleams,
We chase the tide of silly dreams.
In every glance, a secret shared,
With every smile, we are ensnared.

Through fields of whimsy, we shall roam,
With friends beside, we feel at home.
In playful banter, hearts ignite,
Together in this joyful flight.

With tickled ribs and merry cheer,
We dance away each trace of fear.
In every moment, pure and bright,
A map to laughter is our light.

So take my hand; let's run away,
To where the silly games will play.
With every laugh, life's colors flow,
In this wild journey, let us grow.

The Garden of Us

In blooms of hope, our love takes root,
Among the dreams, we gently salute.
Petals soft, in colors bright,
Nurtured by warmth, shielded from night.

With every step on this sacred ground,
Our hearts in rhythm, a love profound.
Through seasons turn, we cultivate,
In this garden, we elevate.

Amongst the thorns, our strength will rise,
In whispered vows beneath the skies.
Sunlight dances on our skin,
In this space, we both begin.

Each raindrop sings a tender tune,
As starry nights give way to June.
Together bloom, we intertwine,
In this fragrant garden, you are mine.

So let us sow with hearts so brave,
In love's embrace, we both are saved.
With every chance, our spirits soar,
In this garden of us, forevermore.

Sailing into Serendipity

With winds of fate, we set our course,
On waters calm, we feel the force.
Each wave a whisper, soft and sweet,
In endless blue, our hearts will meet.

The sun dips low, painting the sea,
A canvas wild for you and me.
With laughter loud, we catch the breeze,
In this journey, we find ease.

Through stormy nights, we'll steer our ship,
On star-lit paths, we take our trip.
In every heartbeat, a story told,
In serendipity, our dreams unfold.

As dolphins dance beneath the waves,
In this adventure, love enslaves.
With every tide, we drift and glide,
Together on this wondrous ride.

So raise the sails; let's chase the light,
Into horizons, futures bright.
In every heartbeat, we are free,
Sailing forth into serendipity.

Threads of Connection

In the quiet hour we meet,
With whispers soft, our hearts greet.
Each moment shared, a gentle thread,
Binding souls with love widespread.

Through laughter bright and tears we find,
A tapestry that fate designed.
In every glance, a story spun,
Connecting two, now always one.

Through days of sun and nights of rain,
We weave a bond through joy and pain.
Each memory a stitch so fine,
Creating life, a love divine.

As seasons change, our roots grow deep,
In every promise, love we keep.
The threads we hold, both strong and true,
Forever stitched, just me and you.

With each new dawn, our hearts will dance,
In every moment, a second chance.
These threads of gold will not unwind,
For in this weave, our lives combined.

Through the Garden of Love

In a garden where dreams bloom bright,
Petals whisper in soft twilight.
Each flower tells a tale so sweet,
Of love that makes our hearts complete.

The sun above, a tender glance,
Ignites the spark, our souls' romance.
In fragrant air, our laughter sways,
Creating joy in sunlit rays.

Amongst the roses, we stroll slow,
With every step, our feelings grow.
Hands entwined, we find our way,
In this garden, love will stay.

Through paths where lilacs softly sway,
We cherish every moment, day.
Beneath the stars, our secrets shared,
In this Eden, hearts laid bare.

As seasons shift, the blooms may fade,
But in our hearts, the love we've made.
Together here, forever entwined,
Through the garden, our love defined.

A Tapestry Woven in Trust

Every thread we weave with care,
A tale of love, a bond we share.
In every knot, a promise sealed,
Our hearts revealed, our truths unpeeled.

Throughout the years, a dance so fine,
With colors bright, your hand in mine.
Each moment threads the fabric strong,
In woven trust, where we belong.

As shadows fall and sunlight plays,
Our tapestry grows in countless ways.
With each design, the scars we mend,
In vibrant hues, our hearts transcend.

In storms we faced, the threads won't break,
Together forged, we'll never shake.
A work of art, both bold and true,
A tapestry made for me and you.

In every weave, our life unfolds,
A story rich with love that holds.
With every stitch, we learn and grow,
A tapestry of love to show.

The Voyage of Us

On a ship of dreams, we set our sail,
Through waters calm and storms that hail.
With every wave, our hearts align,
In this voyage, your hand in mine.

Beneath the stars, we chart our course,
With love as our ever-guiding force.
Through tides of change, we will not fade,
For every moment, memories made.

The horizon calls, a bright surprise,
With every leap, we reach the skies.
Through stormy nights, we stand our ground,
In this journey, true love is found.

With every stop, new shores we greet,
In lands unknown, our hearts will meet.
A compass true within our souls,
Together we achieve our goals.

As seasons change, our sails will shift,
In every challenge, we find our gift.
The voyage of us, forever blessed,
In love's embrace, we find our rest.

A Canvas of Kindness

Colors blend in gentle light,
Each stroke whispers of delight.
A heart so warm, a hand so true,
Kindness blooms in shades anew.

We paint with joy, we sing with grace,
Creating love in every space.
Together we rise, hand in hand,
A masterpiece across the land.

Every gesture, a vibrant hue,
In a world where kindness grew.
With every laugh, and every tear,
We color life, we banish fear.

In this canvas, bright and wide,
Hope and love will always guide.
Through every struggle, we remain,
In kindness' embrace, we have gained.

So let us paint, let spirits soar,
Create a world we all adore.
With every heart, let kindness flow,
A canvas of love, a gentle glow.

Blossoming Together

In the garden of our dreams,
Seeds of love sprout gentle beams.
With every touch, and every word,
Together, our hearts are stirred.

Petals open, colors bright,
In harmony, we find our light.
Through storms we grow, both strong and free,
Blossoming together, you and me.

Roots entwined beneath the soil,
In shared moments, no need to toil.
Nurtured by laughter, a sweet refrain,
We flourish in joy, through pleasure and pain.

The sun will rise, the moon will gleam,
In the tapestry of our shared dream.
Hand in hand, we'll face the weather,
In a world made brighter, we blossom together.

So let us dance through seasons' change,
Embracing life, wide and strange.
With every dawn, a fresh start sings,
In love's embrace, our spirit springs.

Reflections of Us

In quiet moments, we stand still,
Mirrored gazes, hearts that thrill.
Echoes of laughter, whispers of trust,
In reflections of us, love's a must.

Through the looking glass, we see,
The stories shared, just you and me.
Layered memories, tender and bright,
In the depth of night, we find our light.

Time flows past in soft embrace,
Every challenge we've come to face.
In every glance, a world unfolds,
Reflections of us, a story told.

With each sunset, dreams arise,
Captured moments beneath the skies.
Through paths unknown, we'll journey on,
In the tapestry of love, we're never gone.

So let us cherish, each glance we share,
In reflections of us, nothing compares.
With every heartbeat, our story grows,
In love's reflection, the beauty flows.

The Foundations of Forever

Strong and steady as the sun,
In our hearts, the journey's begun.
With trust like stone and love's embrace,
We build a life, our sacred space.

Each brick is laid with tender care,
A future bright, a dream to share.
Through trials faced, we work as one,
In the foundations, love's never done.

With laughter echoing through the halls,
In our home, a warmth that calls.
The whispers of dreams, the echoes we find,
In the foundations of forever, love's intertwined.

Together we weather the storms that come,
In the strength of our bond, we are never numb.
For every challenge, we rise above,
In the heart of our home, forever love.

So let's celebrate this life we've grown,
In every moment, we are never alone.
With roots so deep, we'll always strive,
In the foundations of forever, we thrive.

Whispered Vows Beneath the Stars

In quiet night, our secrets bare,
Beneath the glow, we find our care.
The silver light on dreams we share,
Our whispered vows drift in the air.

With every breath, our souls entwined,
The universe, in love, aligned.
Your hand in mine, two hearts combined,
In starlit skies, true peace we find.

The cosmos sings, a gentle tune,
As shadows dance beneath the moon.
With each soft sigh, our hearts commune,
In endless night, we softly swoon.

Promises kept in sacred space,
In love's embrace, we find our place.
Through trials faced, with gentle grace,
Together, life we will embrace.

Our dreams take flight on wings of trust,
In every moment, love is just.
A symphony of hearts, robust,
In whispered vows, we forever must.

The Dance of Togetherness

Two souls converge, in rhythmic flow,
With every step, our spirits glow.
In laughter shared, our joys bestow,
A dance of love that we both know.

With grace we glide on wooden floors,
In tender steps, our hearts explore.
Every glance, a tale it pours,
In this embrace, we seek for more.

In circles wide, we spin and sway,
Each moment lived, we seize the day.
Through melody, we find our way,
In dance of love, forever stay.

Our hearts align, the music plays,
In softest light, our love displays.
With every beat, the night delays,
In sweet togetherness, we blaze.

This dance of life, hand in hand,
A journey cherished, beautifully planned.
Through every step, we understand,
Together always, forever stand.

Hearts in Harmony

In perfect tune, our hearts unite,
Each whispered word, a soft delight.
With every glance, a spark ignites,
In sacred bonds, we find our light.

A melody born of sweet caress,
In laughter shared, we find our best.
Two souls in sync, a lovely quest,
In harmony, we are truly blessed.

The rhythm flows through gentle hands,
In every beat, our love expands.
With trust as strong as shifting sands,
Together, life's great song demands.

In symphony, our passions rise,
With painted skies and endless ties.
Through all of life, as time flies by,
Our hearts will sing, we'll never die.

So let us dance, embrace the sound,
In harmony, our love is found.
With every note, joy knows no bounds,
In perfect peace, we're ever crowned.

Captured Moments of Bliss

In fleeting seconds, love's pure grace,
With every smile, we find our place.
In captured moments, time we trace,
In memories held, we softly embrace.

A tender glance, a fragile sigh,
In quiet wonders, we learn to fly.
The world around, a blurred goodbye,
As joy unfolds beneath the sky.

With laughter bright, like morning dew,
The gentle touch, so fresh, so new.
In fleeting time, our spirits grew,
In every heartbeat, love rings true.

These moments shared, a painted dream,
In love's embrace, we beam and gleam.
Through simple joys, our hearts esteem,
In blissful times, we dare to dream.

So let us hold each memory dear,
In captured bliss, we draw you near.
In every glance, love's light will steer,
Through moments cherished, year by year.

Threads of Togetherness

In quiet moments, hearts entwine,
We weave our dreams, yours and mine.
Through laughter shared, and whispers near,
Our bond grows strong, year by year.

Each thread a memory, soft and bright,
Stitched with hope, it feels so right.
In storms we stand, hand in hand,
Together always, we understand.

The tapestry of life we make,
Colors vibrant, never to break.
With each embrace, we find our place,
In this shared journey, we're bound by grace.

Through trials faced, we stand as one,
Embracing shadows, seeking the sun.
In every challenge, love will show,
The threads of togetherness will grow.

From dawn to dusk, our spirits soar,
In unity's light, we ask for more.
With every moment, our truth we share,
Threads of love, forever rare.

Radiant Routes of Love

Upon the road, we stroll as two,
With every step love shines anew.
In sunlit paths, our laughter plays,
Radiant routes, brightening days.

Through winding trails, we venture forth,
The warmth of love, our true north.
Each glance exchanged, a spark ignites,
Illuminating our starry nights.

We dance through fields of dreams sublime,
With hearts attuned, in perfect rhyme.
In every corner, beauty sleeps,
Radiant love, forever keeps.

Hand in hand, we chase the dawn,
Navigating paths where hope is drawn.
Through every twist, we shall endure,
For love's pure light, it stays secure.

At every junction, we stand tall,
In love's embrace, we never fall.
Together we face what lies ahead,
On radiant routes, our hearts are fed.

Blossoms in Unity

In gardens bright, where flowers bloom,
Colors blend, dispelling gloom.
Each petal soft, a story told,
Blossoms in unity, brave and bold.

From roots below, to skies above,
Every hue whispers of love.
Together we grow, side by side,
In fields of joy, our hearts collide.

Nature's touch, a gentle grace,
In unity, we find our place.
With every breeze, a promise sways,
Blossoms unite in sunlit rays.

Through seasons warm, through winters cold,
A tapestry of life unfolds.
In every fragrance, dreams take flight,
In unity's arms, we find our light.

As petals fall, new buds arise,
Life's cyclical dance, beneath the skies.
Together we thrive, in love's embrace,
Blossoms in unity, time can't erase.

Footprints on Love's Path

Along the shore, where ripples play,
We leave our marks, come what may.
Each footprint tells a tale so true,
On love's path, me and you.

Through shifting sands and gentle waves,
Together we journey, strong and brave.
In every step, a history made,
Footprints of love that never fade.

With every laugh, with every sigh,
We walk through life, you and I.
Hand in hand, hearts open wide,
On love's path, we take each stride.

Through sunlit mornings and starlit nights,
Our souls reflect love's gentle lights.
In every corner, our journeys meet,
Footprints united, love's heartbeat.

When storms arise, and shadows fall,
Together we'll stand, together we'll call.
Our footprints tell of battles fought,
On love's path, our dreams are sought.

Whispers of Wedded Bliss

In the quiet glow of morning light,
Promises spoken, hearts take flight,
Fingers intertwined, a gentle squeeze,
Together facing life with ease.

Laughter dances on the breeze,
A melody that never frees,
With every glance, a story shared,
In this bond, we are ensnared.

Moments sweet, like honey's kiss,
In your arms, I find my bliss,
Through the storms that may arise,
We will stand, as love defies.

Evenings wrapped in soft embrace,
Reflecting on our sacred space,
Dreams entwined like vines that grow,
In your heart, I've found my home.

Together, we will navigate,
With every step, we cultivate,
A life adorned with joy's decree,
In whispers shared, just you and me.

Crossroads of Commitment

At the intersection of our dreams,
We stand together, or so it seems,
Paths diverging, yet hearts align,
In this journey, your hand in mine.

Choices made beneath starlit skies,
With trust as deep as the ocean's ties,
Every heartbeat leads the way,
In this dance of choice, we stay.

From moments small, big dreams take flight,
Through whispered fears in the dark of night,
With every vow, we build our fate,
Love's compass guides, we cannot wait.

Each turn we take, a story unfolds,
A tapestry of love that molds,
In commitment's grasp, we find our place,
A bond that time cannot erase.

So here we are, at life's great gate,
With courage bright, we illuminate,
In the crossroads where two hearts meet,
Together we create our beat.

Navigating the Heart's Compass

In the sea of love, we sail as one,
With stars above, our journey's begun,
Charting the course with faith so true,
In every tide that brings me to you.

Waves may crash and winds may roar,
Yet with you, I fear no shore,
For in this vessel made of dreams,
We navigate with heart's bright beams.

Through storms we face, hand in hand,
Together strong, in love we stand,
An anchor found in tender grace,
In every challenge, we find our place.

The compass spins with every beat,
Your love, my guide, makes life complete,
With laughter echoing through the night,
We find our way, love shining bright.

So let the voyage ever last,
With memories formed, not just the past,
In the depths of love's vast sea,
Together always, just you and me.

The Dance of Two Souls

In the rhythm of love, our hearts entwine,
Two souls dancing in perfect time,
With every step, a story told,
In silent whispers, our love unfolds.

Feet gliding softly across the floor,
Lost in the moment, wanting more,
Eyes that sparkle, conveying dreams,
In this dance, nothing's as it seems.

Through melodies that kiss the night,
We twirl and spin, feeling so right,
With every beat, our spirits soar,
In synchrony, forevermore.

Between the pauses, love's embrace,
In every heartbeat, finding grace,
Together swaying, a gentle sway,
In this dance, we find our way.

As music fades, but hearts still sing,
In this dance of life, love is the wing,
Our souls connect, forever bound,
In the dance of two, we are found.

Pioneers of Partnership

Hand in hand, we tread the way,
Building bridges day by day.
With shared dreams, we boldly strive,
Together, our hopes come alive.

Through trials faced, we stand as one,
In shadows cast, we find the sun.
Voices strong, united in song,
In this journey, we both belong.

With every step, we break new ground,
In the silence, our hearts resound.
Trusting each other, we will grow,
In every challenge, love will show.

As pioneers, we carve our fate,
Together, we create, create.
In our efforts, we weave a tale,
Partnership will never fail.

Through storms and calm, we find our way,
Navigating night, guiding day.
With hands linked, we rise and soar,
In partnership, we'll seek for more.

Building Dreams Together

With whispers soft, we share our dreams,
In unity, everything redeems.
Brick by brick, we lay the plan,
Together, no limits can span.

Each vision bright, a golden thread,
In harmony, our hearts are fed.
We sketch the future, bold and clear,
In laughter shared, we conquer fear.

Through trials faced, we stand side by side,
With every flaw, our love won't hide.
We lift each other, reaching high,
In a bond that can't deny.

As seasons change, let dreams unfold,
In warmth of hope, our lives behold.
Together we'll brave the wild unknown,
In every challenge, our strength is grown.

With hands united, we build our fate,
In every corner, love calls great.
Through every storm, we find our light,
Building dreams with hearts so bright.

The Magic of Togetherness

In gentle moments, magic spins,
With every smile, the journey begins.
Together, laughter fills the air,
In shared silence, we find our prayer.

Through every tear, we find our grace,
In each embrace, a warm place.
With whispered truths, we break the night,
In togetherness, our hearts take flight.

With dreams entwined, we build and weave,
In every moment, we believe.
In every glance, a story told,
In magic found, we are consoled.

Through every storm, hand in hand,
In the chaos, together we'll stand.
With hearts aligned, a symphony plays,
In love's embrace, we find our ways.

In twilight's glow, we reflect and share,
With every heartbeat, love is rare.
Together, we dance, our spirits blend,
In this magic, there's no end.

In the Embrace of Affection

In gentle warmth, our hearts collide,
With every touch, we set aside.
In the embrace of affection true,
Life blooms brightly, me and you.

Through whispered hopes and sweet caress,
In unity, we find our rest.
In every glance, a promise made,
In love's soft glow, our fears will fade.

With laughter shared, we light the night,
In tender moments, love takes flight.
Through trials faced, we stand so tall,
In affection's arms, we conquer all.

With every heartbeat, rhythms blend,
In this journey, we transcend.
In the embrace, all doubts take flight,
In love's circle, we ignite.

Through seasons change, we'll always stay,
In strong embrace, we'll find our way.
With every kiss, our souls align,
In affection's glow, we forever shine.

The Canvas of Companionable Dreams

In the twilight glow of gentle hues,
We paint our thoughts on the evening views.
Each stroke a whisper, each color a song,
In the gallery of night, we both belong.

Beneath the stars, our visions unite,
Creating a tapestry, woven in light.
With laughter as brush, and love as the frame,
We'll alight the world with our shared flame.

The canvas expands, with every embrace,
In this boundless space, we carve our place.
With the moon as our muse, and dreams as our guide,
We journey together, side by side.

In strokes of passion, and splashes of hope,
We weave our fate, learning to cope.
Each sunset a promise, each dawn a chance,
On this canvas of dreams, we twirl and dance.

So let us create, with colors so bright,
A masterpiece painted in love's pure light.
For in every heartbeats, our visions can gleam,
On this canvas of life, we chase our dream.

Sculpting Our Forever

With chisels of moments, we shape our days,
In the block of existence, each touch conveys.
Sculpting our future with love and with care,
Every facet we carve, a tale we share.

The stone may be rough, but our hands are true,
Molding our dreams into something anew.
In patience and passion, we sculpt time's flow,
Creating a bond that continues to grow.

Each whisper of hope, like a gentle caress,
Guiding the form, in this tender process,
With every detail, we etch in our heart,
A masterpiece born from two lives, not apart.

As seasons will change, and time will unfold,
We'll craft our forever, with visions bold.
Together we'll stand, where the shadows play,
Sculpting our lives in a dance of the clay.

In the gallery of moments, our love is the art,
With every creation, we're never apart.
For in every sculpture, a piece of us stays,
In this timeless journey, our passion displays.

Streams of Shared Aspirations

In the river of dreams, we flow side by side,
Navigating currents where hopes coincide.
The water reflects what our spirits desire,
In the whispers of waves, we fuel the fire.

With hands intertwined, we paddle along,
In the harmonious rhythm, where we both belong.
Each ripple a promise, each splash a cheer,
In this stream of life, we shed every fear.

As the shores of our visions begin to embrace,
We'll wander together, no need for a trace.
With compass of hearts and sails made of trust,
We'll journey together; in love, we adjust.

The future cascades like a waterfall bright,
In the streams of our spirits, we find our light.
With laughter like bubbles, and dreams that ignite,
We'll flow through the valleys, by day and by night.

So let us embark on this river so wide,
Where every desire finds space to reside.
In the waters of life, our aspirations gleam,
In this beautiful voyage, we live our dream.

The Melodies of Merged Lives

In the symphony of us, harmonies blend,
Each note a memory, every chord a friend.
The melody swells, as our hearts take flight,
Dancing to rhythms beneath the moonlight.

With laughter as percussion, and love as the guide,
We compose our journey, with arms open wide.
Each pause an embrace, each rest a sweet sigh,
In the concert of life, we soar to the sky.

When dissonance whispers, we'll find our tune,
Transforming the shadows with light from the moon.
Together we'll flourish, in crescendos we thrive,
In the music of moments, our spirits alive.

As the orchestra plays, in a vibrant embrace,
We'll write our own anthem, each note taking space.
With hearts as our instruments, we'll play every line,
In the rich tapestry where our souls intertwine.

So let us create in this sonorous bliss,
Composing our love with each heartfelt kiss.
For in every heartbeat, our symphony thrives,
In the melodies sung, we find our lives.

The Canvas of Forever

Brushstrokes of time, bold yet fine,
A tapestry woven, with dreams that shine.
Colors of memories dance in the light,
Each moment a whisper, a spark in the night.

The horizon beckons with stories untold,
In hues of the twilight, adventures unfold.
With every heartbeat, a canvas anew,
The masterpiece growing with each breath we do.

Stars twinkle softly, like secrets unfurled,
Each one a promise in this vast, wide world.
The paintbrush of fate, it moves with grace,
Creating our story in this timeless space.

Time drips like honey, sweet and slow,
Every second a gem that we treasure and know.
In the gallery of life, we find our way,
Crafting forever in the light of the day.

So let us embrace the colors so bright,
In the canvas of forever, we find our light.
With each stroke, we gather, create and explore,
Living our dreams forever, forevermore.

Sunlit Promises

Golden rays shimmer on dew-kissed grass,
Whispers of dawn as the moments pass.
In the warmth of the sun, hopes take flight,
Painting the world in vibrant delight.

Children's laughter rings out in the air,
A melody crafted with tender care.
Promises linger in every sweet smile,
In the glow of the sun, we dream for a while.

Fields stretch like oceans, endless and wide,
Each blade of grass, a secret to hide.
The gentle breeze carries wishes on high,
As we dance in the light, underneath the sky.

Moments like petals fall soft on the ground,
Each one a treasure waiting to be found.
In the warmth of each hug, every tear and laugh,
Sunlit promises brighten our path.

So let us gather the light of today,
And chase all our fears and doubts far away.
In the embrace of the sun, hope does renew,
Sunlit promises binding me and you.

Echoes of Laughter

In the corners of rooms, laughter will swell,
A reminder of stories we willingly tell.
Each chuckle a note in a sweet symphony,
Binding us close in joyous harmony.

The echoes ring softly, long after they fade,
In the halls of our hearts, where memories are made.
With every shared moment, we weave a new thread,
A tapestry bright where the joyous have tread.

Familiar voices dance on the breeze,
Reminding us gently of sweet memories.
The playful banter, the warmth of a grin,
In the echoes of laughter, we all can begin.

So let us gather, in circles of light,
Where laughter resounds, and hope feels so right.
With a wink and a smile, we embrace the night,
In the echoes of laughter, all things feel bright.

These moments will linger, like stars up above,
Each chuckle immortal, a testament of love.
In the echoes, we find all the joy we can share,
Together forever, under memories rare.

Unfolding Destinies

In the quiet dawn, where dreams arise,
Destinies weave beneath the skies.
Paths intertwine, like branches of trees,
Guiding us forward, with whispers and flees.

Every step taken, a choice made clear,
In the tapestry rich, woven thread by thread.
The compass within us points true and bright,
In the journey of life, we chase our own light.

Moments of doubt, like shadows will fall,
But the heart knows the way, it answers the call.
Through valleys of struggle, up mountains of grace,
Unfolding destinies, each at our pace.

So let us embrace every twist and turn,
For through every trial, there's so much to learn.
In the dance with the stars, our spirits will soar,
Unfolding destinies, forever explore.

With every heartbeat, a story untold,
In the book of our lives, each chapter unfolds.
Hand in hand, we journey through time's endless tide,
Unfolding destinies, hearts open wide.

Printed in the USA
CPSIA information can be obtained
at www.ICGtesting.com
CBHW072119221124
17859CB00020B/618